# STEPS TO DESIGN YOUR LIFE

A Powerful Guide to Build Success Mindset, Start Thinking Positive, Conquer Challenges and Achieve Long Term Goals in Life.

PRADIP N DAS

One summer, an ant was living alone, who used to work hard to prepare for winter. The ant made friendship with a grasshopper. The grasshopper was warm, had a full belly of food, and was singing and enjoying life. On the other hand, the ant was hard at work carrying grains and other foodstuffs into its storage. The grasshopper saw the hard-working ant and asked to join him in fun. The ant stopped for a moment and asked the grasshopper, "My friend, I wish to join you, but I am not done yet with my preparations for the winter. Are you prepared for the winter?" The grasshopper smiled and said, "You need to relax a little bit and enjoy the present moment."

The ant worked hard during the summer, collecting food while the grasshopper enjoyed the bright summer days. The grasshopper would look at the ant every day and laugh. "Why do you work so hard, dear ant? Why are you wasting the beautiful summer? Let's enjoy." The ant simply answered, "I am preparing for enough food and a well-built shelter to get me through winter. Are you prepared for the winter?"

The days went by fast, and instead of working and preparing for the winter, the grasshopper preferred to dance and enjoy its leisure. He did not realize that the wonderful summer days will not last forever.

Then, winter arrived, and it became freezing cold, and snow began to fall. This time the winter was very severe. The grasshopper didn't feel like singing and lying around in the open anymore, and it realized that the ant was right about getting prepared. The only option for the grasshopper now was to find warm shelter and get some food. The grasshopper remembered how the ant worked so hard while he kept on enjoying during the summertime.

In the icy chilled weather, the grasshopper felt the need for some help and finally found the ant and its shelter. Before the ant could say anything, the grasshopper started pleading with the ant, "I had not imagined that the winter would be so harsh and that there would be no food. I am extremely sorry that I have not listened to you. I am not prepared, but I have learned my lesson. Please let me in and share some food with me." The ant took the grasshopper in and shared with him everything he had. The grasshopper couldn't believe how much food and how big of a shelter the ant had. He couldn't help questioning him, "Why did you work so much and so hard to build and save up so much of everything, which you alone will definitely not need until the end of winter?" The ant smiled and replied, "My dear friend, do you remember what I have been asking you every day?" The grasshopper looked at the floor and replied, "are you prepared for the winter?" "That's right," said the ant and continued, "Every day when I asked you that question and got your answer, I then decided to prepare myself to help my lazy friend. So I worked twice as much to build a big enough shelter and to have enough food to take you in and help you through the winter."

You are the creator of your own destiny or the artist of your own life. You hold the brush in your hand, design it the way you want it to be, and fill it with colors of joy, happiness, and love, and the image will be so beautiful to gaze at. It is not always the colors we fill that would yield a masterpiece, but we sure would gain experience to include the right colors and shades. Most important is how you want it to look and how you complete the picture.

When I was young, like any other normal village boy, I used to have a daily routine, as usual getting up in the morning, finishing my daily necessities, studying for some time, then playing with friends, going to school, and so on. At that time, I was completely unaware of all these fundamentals of success. I didn't have any idea how to design my life then, but I had the desire at the back of my mind. The desire was to get as much education as I could and find a job that paid well. That goal was attained at age 23 when I joined a big FMCG company.

I continued working in multiple organizations, but there were no drastic changes in life. When I was 45, a thought struck my mind. The thought was to keep working and start writing books to share my experiences and learning.

But, my ultimate goal is to inspire millions of people to live a happy, prosperous and spiritual life and free myself from any obligation, live a happy, healthy and wealthy life, and impact people's lives. In fact, I want to give back to the universe something in return. My first book was published in 2020, and thereafter published a series of books with the intention to transform the lives of people.

## Designing Life Is Not Easy

"What do you want to be when you grow up?" is a question that we constantly ask kids and are expected to have an answer for. But the irony is how kids can decide at an early age what they want to become.

Considering an average lifespan of 75 years, we spend 25 years working, 25 years sleeping, and the remaining 25 years on other activities.

Growth happens throughout life, from a baby to a toddler to a kid to a teen to an adult, but growth doesn't stop there. We continue to experience new experiences every day and grow with those.

Once you commit to taking the step forward in faith, you begin entering into an authentic and intentional life - that is when you start designing your own life.

Just how an artist design's life, one needs to visualize the goals in their life and plan accordingly to achieve the end outcome.

You first have to imagine that it can come true and then changing your life to achieve that. The irony is, while generally happy, many of us have a life, not of our own design.

*"Whatever the mind can conceive and believe, the mind can achieve."* -
*Napoleon Hill*

An architect design a building by first laying out the blueprints. The house emerges from a sheet of drawings. A writer outlines a book with a table of contents. The book takes shape from the imagination of the writer. The creation from scratch is real work. Is it possible to really design your own life in much the same way the architect designs a house and the writer designs a book? Certain things in life, such as upbringing, education, childhood times, parent, etc., happened before you came to know the ability to design your life. All that happened in the past has shaped who you are today, so you need to start designing your life from this point forward.

Since we cannot control the past, we can make a plan today and work on our plan each day, we can modify our plan as necessary, and we can make the best of what shows up even when it is not what we want.

*The blueprint*

The blueprint is very important. The blueprint for your life can be the architect's house design, the author's table of contents, or a business plan. You set out certain goals and map out a plan of action on how you will get to each one. Maybe you start with your ideal career and strategize how you will reach there from where you are at present. Then you can design your personal life, relationships, hobbies, etc.

*The mindset*

You need to get into the right mindset after making the blueprint. The power of your thoughts, positive success mindset, and focus on your goals will improve your chances of success. You must believe in yourself and your ability to achieve your goals. You must become aware of your thoughts and maintain the ones that will support you in getting what you want.

*The Actions*

Once the blueprint and the right mindset are in place, you must take the actions necessary to build your life as you desire it. Just keep following the action steps you outlined in your blueprint.

*The Assessment*

Actions need to be monitored regularly to check on your progress. You should keep monitoring your progress toward your goals to stay motivated. Celebrate the small wins on your way toward your bigger goals. Each win is one step closer to your ultimate life design.

*The Improvement*

Make necessary corrections, corrective actions, reassess your actions and monitor the progress of your goals. Review the action plan periodically and update it as things progress. Then establish some new actions that will get you back on the path, even if it's a different route.

## Frameworks

The main intent of writing this book is to make a concise guideline for the strategy to be adopted to design life towards success from an early age. Most middle-aged people face many challenges in their personal and professional lives due to a lack of direction, planning, certain habits and techniques, which ultimately limit their productivity and success. This book aims to show readers how design thinking can help us create a meaningful and fulfilling life regardless of who or where you are, what you have done for a living so far in your life.

The same design elements help you to build your career and your life. Your life can be overflowing with fulfillment and joy, along with being more creative and productive. The self-talk, the growth mindset, the risk-taking, accept mistakes, learn and apply, create new habits, think abundance, think long term, think positive... all these fundamentals when engrossed in mind from early ages of life with ready tools and techniques become highly productive and could bring miracles in life.

In the subsequent chapters, all these fundamental elements to designing life will be described in detail, along with action points for each element to facilitate learning and easy implementation. This book will certainly work as a handbook and will be highly supportive for people to become successful, guide them to follow the right path in achieving all goals in their life and make their life happy.

*"True abundance isn't based on our net worth, it's based on our self-worth."—*
*Gabrielle Bernstein*

You might have heard the Tomato story. Just find a tomato from your kitchen or the store, cut open the tomato, count the number of seeds, and assume 50 seeds. These numbers are the potential tomato plants. Assume each plant produces 50 tomatoes. Multiply the number of seeds (potential plants) by the number of tomatoes, i.e., 50 seeds x 50 tomatoes = 2500 potential tomato plants. These 2500 potential plants will produce 50 tomatoes, each having 50 seeds. So, one tomato will produce 125000 (2500 x 50) tomatoes in the next generation and 6,250,000 (125,000 x 50) potential tomato plants.

One little tomato, no more than 3 cm in diameter, holding 50 seeds means there are 50 possibilities in one tomato for future plants. In the fourth generation, this one little tomato has a potential of 6,250,000 tomato plants which have further potentials for future plants!

An abundance mindset means there are enough resources to go around for everyone. But, as pleasant as it sounds, it isn't easy to believe there are great things available, whether it is opportunities, money, food, etc., in the world for all. So, people easily get trapped into the opposite, the scarcity mindset that there is only a finite amount of resources.

When you have the scarcity mindset, you have difficulty sharing recognition and credit or profit and power with those who contributed to the production. It becomes challenging to feel genuinely happy for others' success when you have the scarcity mindset because your mindset plays a major role in how you view the world.

**Benefits of an Abundance Mindset**

More opportunities and wealth are your benefits when you apply the principles of the abundance mindset in the world of business and professional work.

The quality of your relationships is what matters most both in business and professional work.

For business, it is your relationships with your existing and potential customers. As for professional work, it's your relationships with your existing, former, and future coworkers. In the case of business, you are selling a product or service that targets your customers' specific needs and wants.

When you help your buyers solve their problems with your service or product, you form a trusting and healthy relationship.

Applying the abundance mindset, you only sell them the product or service if truly that will help them overcome their immediate problem. You won't force the sale just to make money even though you know your product or service won't help.

Knowing there are plenty of people out there who will be a great fit for your product or service, you have no problem letting go of people who are not.

In the case of professional work, you understand your value as a worker. You help the company grow and generate revenue while helping your colleagues.

Not viewing others' success as intimidating, you are willing to become a team player. Wanting everyone to benefit in the process, you genuinely are willing to help your coworkers.

By creating true value in the company, you become indispensable and are treasured by your company.

Having an abundance mindset allows you to understand that there are many job opportunities in the world. Therefore, even if you are let go from your company, you will soon find another job given your unique skill set and the healthy relationships you have developed in your previous company.

Job competency is important, but more important is how your former and future co-workers feel about working with you.

If your former coworkers did not enjoy working with you, they would not recommend you for future jobs. Your relationships with your coworkers are more important than you think. Genuinely help your colleagues by being an effective team player.

Your professional network will be your most important asset when asking for promotions and applying for new jobs.

Finally, having an abundance mindset creates many opportunities for you. Your ego wants you to compete with others because of your survival instinct. But both of you can benefit from working together. Operating as a team, everyone involved benefits from the result.

Adopting the abundance mindset, you won't act out of desperation, knowing there are endless opportunities. You will gladly show appreciation, recognition, and praise for others' efforts.

## How to Develop an Abundance Mindset?

Instead of looking at situations negatively, you view them as opportunities with a positive perspective. When you live life this way, you understand that life doesn't happen *to* you; rather, it happens *for* you.

Every event is to help you become stronger and more resilient. As a result, your comfort zone expands.

Challenging problems no longer pose as threats because you can now handle them with ease. Give and help others along the way out of generosity and goodwill.

## Action Point

Take a problem not as a threat but as an opportunity because every event in life makes you stronger.

*"If you want life to change, you have to change. If you want life to be better, you have to be better"—Jim Rohn*

You have heard the famous story of tortoise and hare. Despite being slow at the race, the tortoise takes on the challenge and puts itself forward. On the other hand, the hare is very fast compared to the tortoise and overconfident about its own speed. But the fixed mindset causes the tortoise to lose the race. "I'm fast; therefore, I will win even if I take a nap." The tortoise demonstrates a growth mindset. This story is a great example of how the growth mindset can bring surprising results. The same thing happens to most people. If you keep on moving towards your goal, you will reach it, whereas if you have all the skillset but stay in the cocoon of your comfort zone, you will not succeed.

## What is Growth Mindset All About

According to Zimmerman, the most important thing you can do is to embrace a growth mindset. This is the mindset that will allow you to dream big and push the boundaries of your ideas to new levels.

She subscribes to the maxim, "Everything on the way rather than in the way," from leading educator Dr. John Demartini.

Instead of judging experiences in terms of failures and successes, frame them in a positive light. You will have challenges and obstacles along the way. Recognize that all of them can help you grow and become a better person.

Dr. Carol Dweck, professor of psychology at Stanford University, explained that if you aren't in a growth mindset, you probably have a fixed mindset, which is dangerous because it will ultimately stifle your ability to reach new achievements. He also said, "A fixed mindset is when people believe their basic qualities, intelligence, talents, and abilities are just fixed traits. They have a certain amount, and that's that." With a growth mindset, people believe that their talents and abilities can be developed over time through experience and mentorship, so they push themselves and "go for it." "They're not always worried about how smart they are, how they'll look, or what a mistake will mean," Dweck explained. "They challenge themselves and grow."

Alibaba founder Jack Ma failed his college exams thrice, faced ten rejections from Harvard, and was the only candidate to be rejected by KFC amongst twenty-three people. That is when he founded Alibaba- the company which was in great loss for many years, and after 25 years of immense struggle, Alibaba is highly successful in present years.

Nike, the famous top sports shoe company, strongly believes in innovation, great performance, sustainability, authenticity, and customization. These factors prove that the company takes great care of its' clients and has a growth mindset that leads them towards a top-ranking company.

A growth mindset imbibed people, permanently improve their intelligence and ability to learn new skills through hard work, training, and perseverance. They believe that learning is a continuous process. They accept and even welcome failure as a means to move forward. In fact, the benefits of this growth mindset are substantial. It makes relationships between people much better, working as a team with the knowledge they have to learn together.[1]

When you train your brain towards growth, your body and soul work

---

[1] www. entrepreneur.com

double-time to achieve it. A person whose early life has been easy takes extra effort to excel later in life. The sight of an obstacle force you to make a U-turn if you have not faced any challenges in early life.

My school teacher taught me an important lesson: if you are escaping from the challenge today, you will have to do the same for the rest of your life. That one piece of advice still rings in my ear. Without challenges, life is just bland. Look at problems as blessings and learn from them. All you need to do is change your attitude towards it. It is just a decision you make at this moment.

A productive mindset enables you to value what you are doing, regardless of the outcome. It helps you handle problems, chart new opportunities, and work on more critical business issues. It focuses on growth and constant improvement.

Growth is off the table if you have a fixed mindset. Your intelligence, skills, or talents are in static mode. Small business owners who have a fixed mindset care about their reputation, generally at the expense of the business. They believe that they are more superior to others.

Nokia, a renowned mobile manufacturing company that refused to upgrade its' mobiles to the Android platform, was what its' competitors, such as Samsung, adapted and became much stronger. Hence, Nokia had to face a stiff downfall.

A growth mindset is when a person believes that it is possible to improve his/her intelligence. At the same time, a fixed mindset is when a person believes that he/she can't get any more intelligent.

A growth mindset allows for growing pains, failures, and mistakes. A fixed mindset, on the other hand, says your performance is already predetermined. Thus, the philosophy of a fixed mindset declares that if you fail once, you must not have the innate qualities for such an undertaking.

The best example of a growth mindset is "I wonder what would happen if I tried it this way." A growth mindset is playing, and a fixed mindset is working.

If you have a fixed mindset, you believe that your intelligence and talents are unchangeable. This means you may feel like the only way to excel is to conform to someone else's standard - that nothing will ever change. You may also believe that failure is due to not having the right skills or working hard enough rather than just having a tough day or taking on too much responsibility. If you have a growth mindset, you will pay more attention to your tasks and find satisfaction in being better at them. You will also be happier about other things in your life - for example, getting along with your colleagues and feeling good about yourself as a person.

## How to Develop Growth Mindset

You can develop a growth mindset in yourself if you wish to do. Following are some of the tips to develop a growth mindset-

*Focus on learning*

Every situation offers a learning opportunity and an outlet to become better in the long run. There are ample examples of people making it through hard times and coming out polished and more complete than they ever were before. You develop your growth mindset when you learn new things and improve your skills or acquire new skills. You should be on the lookout for opportunities to learn. You will also want to ask and explore what others think about topics such as how we learn and what makes us happy. To function effectively in this rapidly changing world, you need to learn new things to remain valuable. Continuous lifelong learning will help you to adapt to all changes. When you are always learning, you will more easily step out of your comfort zone and grow in your career. Besides, learning new things gives you a feeling of accomplishment, which, in turn, boosts your confidence in your capabilities. You feel more ready to take on challenges and succeed.

*Take ownership*

Ownership is the mentality that stimulates and causes enthusiasm. Ownership is a feeling; it cannot be delegated. An ownership mindset is the willingness to think big and deliver better and in a manner that adds to one's reputation. When you take ownership, you try harder and are more willing to take on new challenges. You realize that these challenges can make them better at what they do. It makes a big difference in shaping your career and your success. Ownership means delivering a continuous improvement of your performance—ownership results in improved motivation, enthusiasm, and greater commitment.

*Take risks*

It is essential to take a risk and follow our intuition and simply take action. It may not be perfect, but we keep on improvising and learning from our mistakes and correct them accordingly. Mistakes and failures are part of the game. Most successful people fail more than they win, but they never shy away from taking decisions and actions. When you take risks and get better at taking them from an early age, you will also learn how to take risks in your adult life. Most of the successful people in the world are risk-takers. They take many risks in their way to achieve success. Their grit and determination increased many folds by taking a risk to make that work happen. To climb the ladder of success, you must be actively involved and must be willing to take the risk.

## Change yourself

Jim Rohn said, "If you want life to change, you have to change. If you want life to be better, you have to be better". No one has an ability or skill that is fixed. Everyone changes over time. You may think, "I'm not very good at singing" or "I will never be a good swimmer," but those can be changed. If you bring positivity to your life and make constructive changes, you will be happier, brighter, and more successful. It is certainly a state of mind that is well worth developing.

## Start asking questions

you need to ask questions such as: "What do you want? What is your goal? What is bothering you? What makes you afraid? What can you do to overcome this?" Finding answers to these questions will be the first step to rebuild your self-belief. During the process, you should be conscious of working towards your goals and pushing away low self-esteem. When you start asking questions, you get to answer yourself. Asking questions is one of the most effective ways to find the right direction to go forward.

In short, having a growth mindset will help you to improve your performance and make you happier. A growth mindset helps to see the positive side of what has happened during setbacks and failures.

**Action Point**

The most important action for improving the growth mindset is to take ownership.

# 6.    Focus on long term

*"Keep your eyes focused on your long-term goals. Even if you make a mistake, get back on track and keep moving."*        *– Esse Dagogo*

The story of the king of wealth Warren Buffett is very inspiring. It is true that Warren Buffett didn't start making huge money until he hit his 50s. In fact, about 99.7% of his wealth has been earned after his 52nd birthday.

When he was 11 years old, he started buying stock. He filed his first tax return, delivered newspapers, and owned multiple pinball machines placed in various businesses when he was a teenager. When he graduated, he already owned a stake in a forty-acre farm.

He was a natural-born entrepreneur who had an unreasonable approach to creating his wealth over the years.

In 1982, Forbes printed the first list of the 400 richest Americans. Buffett has been on the list every single year since the magazine's existence. During his first time, he was listed with a net worth of $250 million. Three years later, he quadrupled that number. And in 1989, he was worth $3.6 billion — more than tripling his $1 billion in just four years!

As of July 2018, Buffett's net worth is $86.6 billion per Forbes. And believe it or not, even though he has an eleven-figure income, he draws a salary of only $100,000 at Berkshire Hathaway and spends it frugally.

How did he increase his wealth by so much and so fast? In the broadest of explanations, he invested wisely in real assets that produced a positive cash flow for him each month, and he kept his expenses to the minimum that left him more savings to keep investing.

Success is not going to come to you overnight. Most of the great success you heard about are created in years. Skills are built over the years, so think long-term to achieve your work, career, and money goals.

In one of his commercials, Lionel Messi said, "It took me 17 years and 144 days to become an overnight success." If you want to achieve great success in life, you must aim for the long term. Not the short-term, not days, not weeks, and not months.

And this is one of the most common challenges most people face – they don't want to wait for the long-term; they want quick and easy fixes. And this is why most people are not successful.

Things that come quick and easy will not last long. Things that are hard to come by or require your long-term effort to achieve will give you the most reward.

Everyone knows that exercise is good and keeps you healthy over the long term, but most people choose to ignore it because they simply fail to see the long-term reward.

The thing is that people fail to persist in the long term. When those people started doing physical exercise, they wanted quick results.

They exercise only for a few weeks or months, and then they get distracted and move over to another activity or give up on their exercise.

Never let this happen to your dreams and goals. One of the key success mindsets is your ability to focus on the long-term. When it comes to success, don't think in terms of a few months; think in terms of years. Hold on to your vision and work on it relentlessly. Bill Gates once said, "Most people overestimate what they can do in one year and underestimate what they can do in ten years." So, think long-term. Prepare yourself to play the long-term game, not the short-term one.

Actually, the journey to success is not crowded because most people give up on their way there.

## How to Focus on Long Term

*Break Your Long Term Goal*

How do you eat an elephant? The answer is one bite at a time. When you have a large goal that you are working on, breaking it down into small bite-size pieces will help you stay consistent. For example, your goal is to become a successful digital coach that provides you with a sufficient income to allow you to work exclusively from home. To succeed, you take your main or larger goal and break it down into small pieces, and you have something you can work on every day.

By breaking your larger goal down into small bite-size pieces, you can give yourself little wins. Those little wins will give you the motivation you need to keep going and stay focused on long-term goals.

*Make a habit of working toward your goal*

Successful entrepreneurs take a little step forward every day. The more you work at something, the easier it becomes. You are so focused on the daily grind of working through the smaller tasks that move you towards your goal that you forget what you are working towards.

It is important to make that connection between today's activities and what you are trying to achieve. Take some time regularly to connect what you are doing right now with those long-term goals.

Develop a thick skin

It is important to ignore the negative comments. No one is perfect. Learn to accept constructive criticism from your peers. No matter how well your business is performing, someone will always be there to offer both constructive criticism and negative comments. You need to filter out the negative comments and focus on the former.

*Focus on the Process, Not Results*

By focusing on the process instead of the results, we see immediate progress. Let's say your goal is to get in shape. You go walking every morning. Initially, you have difficulty getting up in the early morning and feel reluctant to leave the bed. However, this will be routinized at the end of two weeks; you will start enjoying it and feel energized. Focusing on the process of consistently going for a morning walk motivates you to continue pursuing your goal.

*Be Consistent*

Consistency is key to achieving any goal. If you are not consistently working on your goal, you will fail. Try to do something every day towards meeting your goal. The key is to do something consistently and regularly.

## Action Point

Perform daily activities by breaking long-term goals into short-term goals and then into daily goals.

*"Our attitude towards life determines life's attitude towards us." – John Mitchell*

He slowly figured out how to live a full life without limbs, adjusting to what healthy people accomplish without thinking. He writes with two toes on his left foot and a special grip that slid onto his big toe. He knows how to use a computer and can type up to 45 words per minute using the "heel and toe" method. He has also learned to throw tennis balls, play drum pedals, get a glass of water, comb his hair, brush his teeth, answer the phone and shave. He also plays golf, and he has even Skydived.

He has traveled to over 57 countries giving motivational speeches to millions of people. He believes in sharing the gospel of hope and salvation with them and inspiring them to be the best version of themselves that they can be with the help of God.

You probably guessed who he is. He is none other than Nick Vujicic, one of the greatest inspiratory. Nick was born in 1982 in Melbourne, Australia, without arms and legs. Throughout his childhood, Nick not only dealt with the typical challenges of school and adolescence, but he also struggled with depression and loneliness. He tried to drown himself at age 10 because of a bully at school. His love for his parents prevented him from actually doing the deed.

According to Nick, the victory over his struggles, as well as his strength and passion for life today, can be credited to his faith in God. His family, friends, and the many people he has encountered along the journey have inspired him to carry on, as well.

He has saved and transformed the lives of countless people who were depressed and thought about suicide; people with disabilities who thought that they had no purpose, who didn't have the chance to be happy in life. They thought they had no chance, but Nick has inspired them all. He is given hope to millions of people worldwide.

This is only possible when a person thinks positively. He can encounter any challenge if the positivity is strong and powerful enough.

Think about multinational Fast Food Joint KFC Colonel Sanders. One of the most amazing aspects of his life is that when he reached the age of sixty-five, Harland Sanders found himself penniless after running a restaurant for several years. He retired and received his first social security check, which was for one hundred and five dollars. And that was just the beginning of his international fame and financial success story.

Col. Sanders was a fellow who really loved to share his fried chicken recipe. He had a lot of positive influence from those who tasted the chicken. Now, the Colonel was retired and up in age, and while most people believed in the sanctimony of retirement, the Colonel opted to conquer the world with his cool new chicken recipe. With little means at his disposal, Colonel Sanders traveled door to door to houses and restaurants all over his local area. He wanted to partner with someone to help promote his chicken recipe. Needless to say, he was met with little enthusiasm.

He started traveling by car to different restaurants and cooked his fried chicken on the spot for restaurant owners. If the owner liked the chicken, they would enter into a handshake agreement to sell the Colonel's chicken. Legend has it that Colonel Sanders heard 1009 "no"s before hearing his first "yes."

Colonel in front of his first KFC store. The deal was that for each piece of chicken the restaurant sold, Sanders would receive a nickel. The restaurant would receive packets of Colonel's secret herbs and spices in order to avoid them knowing the recipe. By 1964, Colonel Sanders had 600 franchises selling his trademark chicken. At this time, he sold his company for $2 million but remained as a spokesperson. In 1976, the Colonel was ranked as the world's second most recognizable celebrity.

It's amazing how the man started at the age of 65, when most retire, and built a global empire out of fried chicken.

Another important success mindset you need to develop is optimism. You must look at everything you do from a positive side rather than the negative side.

Think about it, if you believe that the economy is going down and you have a new product to launch, are you going to launch it?

Jack Ma, the founder of Alibaba and one of the wealthiest men in China, once said in a seminar that successful people are extremely optimistic.

They believe that the future will be better than it is now, and that is why they continue to invest and produce better products and services in their companies.

Jack Ma started Alibaba because he believed the internet is going to be the future. He is extremely positive about e-commerce and strongly believes that online shopping is the future. And that is what lead him to start Alibaba.

If Ma were a pessimist, he would never have done it.

Think about what will happen to your business or life if you constantly worry about a market crash, jobs lost, economic recession, failures, etc.

So, be positive. Everything may not be good, but there is definitely something good in everything, and focus on those.

My friend, you can't live a positive life if you constantly complain and litter negativity in your life.

Someone negative will find it hard to achieve great success in life because he constantly focuses on what can go wrong rather than what can go right.

When you think about the negatives, you will feel the fears and eventually stop taking action.

So, instead of letting the negative stop you, choose to focus on the positives. What if you succeed? What if you achieve your goals?

What if you become rich? What kind of life do you want to live? Where do you want to have your next vacation?

Focus on the positive and let the excitement of achievement drive you rather than shunning yourself from the negatives.

Believe. Give your best shot, and you will eventually have either of the two outcomes. If you succeed, you make a milestone in life; you learn a lesson if you fail. Be positive, try, have no regret.

**Action Point**

Leave aside negative thoughts, focus on positives and give your best try.

# 8.  Improve Risk-Taking Abilities

*"The person who risks nothing, does nothing, has nothing, is nothing, and becomes nothing. He may avoid suffering and sorrow, but he simply cannot learn and feel and change and grow and love and live." - Leo F. Buscaglia*

Now, imagine you are asked to speak at an event, but you dislike being in front of crowds. Do you make up an excuse and decline, or rise to the occasion, and start thinking about how you'll prepare? How you respond says a lot about your overall success in life.

If you are not taking risks in your career, you might actually be creating more risk for yourself. Suppose you are not pushing the limits of your career comfort zone -- by considering bold moves like a role in a different functional area, proposing a new idea. In that case, you are not exploiting the full capacity of your career growth.

## Risk to Grow

The legendary boxer Muhammad Ali said, "He who is not courageous enough to take risks will accomplish nothing in life."

"I don't want to risk it!" How many times have you said that or thought it? So, you don't stand up for yourself or ask for what you want; maybe you think wistfully of your life dream but never take action. And in the meantime, life goes on, and our precious time ticks away... "Fortune favors the bold!"

Risk puts you in charge instead of waiting for life to come at you. When you risk, you will grow, whether you achieve what you want or not. You will learn, and you will become more fearless. Every time you take a chance, you expand your personality and sphere of influence in the world. Invite people to your risk. It builds bonds.

Nobody can ever say with 100 percent certainty that an idea will succeed, but they will be able to know only after trying that idea. By learning how to overcome the fear of failure that comes with risk-taking, you can perhaps reach your greatest height. You become more focused, determined, and persistent when you take a risk, key traits for leadership roles.

## Never Overestimate Risk and Underestimate the Opportunity

We tend to overestimate risk and underestimate opportunity. It is natural to focus heavily on the negative consequences of what might go wrong. Many people tend to underestimate the ability to handle the consequences of risk while discounting the cost of taking no action, which leads them to settle for sticking to the status quo.

Underestimating a risk that eventually becomes a reality can lead to losses. Overestimating risk is common too. At times, we exaggerate and go well out of our way to avoid risks... even those with very low probability. This obviously comes at a cost, i.e., sacrificing a chance to earn decent rewards.

A second key reason for overestimating risk is that there are few negative consequences for estimating too highly, whilst a low estimation of risk can be disastrous on all fronts. It might mean there is much paperwork, and sometimes more input is necessitated, but practitioners seem willing to accept these consequences.

## Action Point

The most important action for improving the ability to take risks is to be courageous and never overestimate risk and underestimate the opportunities.

*"It takes guts and humility to admit mistakes. Admitting we're wrong is courage, not weakness." - Roy T. Bennett*

Robin has become an entrepreneur with more than $10 million turnovers in two years. He confessed what transpired to him when he was invited to his college convocation.

Robin joined an engineering college, whereas his father wanted him to become Indian Administrative Service (IAS) Officer. Robin was very introverted and was ridiculed by his classmates and seniors. He did not do well in his studies because his dad asked him to appear for IAS again, and he spent his time preparing for them. During the 4th semester, his mother passed away. He cried for days because his mother was the only one who understood him. His attendance in the college remained low, and even the principal rebuked him for the low attendance. His friends always ridiculed him because he was a loser. He did not laugh at their jokes, but he started drinking and developed several bad habits to mix with them.

He remained unsuccessful in getting a job, whereas all his classmates got placed through campus interviews. He had tried a lot, attended English speaking classes, and brought new pair of a shirt. His father considered him as a spoiled child and saw no hope. But this time, he is very much determined as he had promised his mom that he would shine one day.

He started doing private tuitions and preparing for CAT. He got 99.87 percentile but couldn't make it again to a big IIM because of his low grades. He finally got admitted into a decent management college, and a helpful bank manager arranged for the loan. After passing out, he joined a good MNC, but he did not last for 3 months because of being inefficient.

Then he started making iPhone apps in his leisure time while he was applying to a few companies. Slowly, he took it up as a more serious start-up and got hold of two more friends like him who were from an electronics background and unable to find a job.

Within six months, he hired a small office and had a small group of 8 engineers working with him. He bagged several contracts from various mobile companies, and the workforce increased to 80 developers, and within the year, he has reached break-even.

At this juncture, Robin thanked God for his blessings. He even thanked that senior who ragged him on his first day at college, his professors who ridiculed him, and the

numerous friends who took him as a loser.
My advice to all students is to shine in life. If
I can, you can.

## Mistakes Are Necessary

In my opinion, mistakes are a good
thing. You can't grow if you don't allow
yourself to make mistakes. The trick is to
focus on what you learned from the mistake
and how to improve from it.

It is useless to agonize over the past
because we can't change them. You just need
to recognize that you simply made a mistake.
You learned something valuable from it and
can now move forwards. It means you can
focus on a solution and be far further ahead
than if you'd never allowed yourself to make
a mistake.

If you want to be genuinely successful
in both work and life, you have to be willing
to set aside your pride, your fears. The

journey toward earning respect begins the moment you recognize your mistakes.

Hopefully, by being honest and humble about the small mistakes we make, we avoid big, disastrous mistakes, and the respect we get from owning up to a mistake extends into virtually every professional environment. So admitting when you were wrong doesn't make you weak – it makes you professionals.

Mistakes happen in our life to teach some important lessons. It is important to analyze the lesson which the almighty wants to convey through that mistake. Prudence lies in taking the lesson seriously and implementing the teachings in our life ahead.

Accepting your mistakes means you are taking responsibility for your actions. You are accepting that you are capable of making mistakes which is very human. You will realize that you need to improve on a particular thing and learn from it, eventually becoming a better person. So it is always good to accept your mistake.

## Take Complete Responsibility

A mindset for success means being able to take responsibility for all that you do, whether good or bad.

If you make a mistake or harm someone along your path, taking responsibility lets, you contain the damage and preserve your reputation. It also encourages you to think about how you could avoid that mistake in the future.

Likewise, if you accomplish something, you have to claim responsibility for it. Only then will others realize what you can do and support you on your path to success.

## How to Approach Mistake

Even the most successful people have made blunders in their life, but the main point is that they didn't repeat them. We all make mistakes, some accept, and some don't. So whenever you realize that you have made some mistake, do self-talk explaining it is common to make mistakes. These mistakes we commit are the life experiences from which we mold ourselves to a better version of who we are.

Every time the thought comes back, simply remind yourself that you have already been forgiven, so there's no reason to feel bad anymore. The faster you can forgive yourself and let things go, the faster you'll be able to get on with your life.

Finally, we should acknowledge and embrace our mistakes because they are part of our life journey. We reach our ideal life once we realize what does not work and what we should avoid. Instead of viewing mistakes as failures, we should see them as growth opportunities. If we keep making the same mistakes, this shows us where we need to grow and improve. Most people hide from their weaknesses, and they deny themselves the chance to grow and live the life they want.

**Action Point**

Learn from the mistake and ensure not to repeat the same mistake.

A very strong woodcutter once joined a job with a timber merchant. The woodcutter was determined to do his best as the work conditions and salary was good. The Timber merchant owner gave him an ax and showed him where he was supposed to work. On the first day, the woodcutter brought 18 trees down.

The merchant owner was very happy. "Congratulations," he said. "Go on that way!" Very motivated by these words, the woodcutter tried harder the next day, but he only could bring down 15 trees. The third day he tried even harder, but he only could bring down 10 trees. Day after day, he was bringing down fewer and fewer trees.

"I must be losing my strength," the woodcutter thought. He went to the merchant owner and apologized, saying that he could not understand what was happening.

"When was the last time you sharpened your ax?" the timber owner asked. "Sharpen? I had no time to sharpen my ax. I have been very busy trying to cut trees...."

To get optimal results, we need to sharpen our skills consistently. Being proficient at our job can help us achieve our targets.

## Why Learning?

Learning is very much essential to our existence. Just like food nourishes our bodies, learning nourishes our minds. Continuous learning is necessary for acquiring knowledge and competencies to expand skillsets and develop future opportunities. It forms part of your personal and professional development to avoid stagnation and reach your full potential. To function effectively in this rapidly changing world, you need to learn new things to remain valuable. Lifelong learning will help you to adapt to all changes. When you're always learning, you will more easily step out of your comfort zone and grow in your career. Besides, learning new things gives you a feeling of accomplishment that, in turn, boosts your confidence in your capabilities; you feel more ready to take on challenges and succeed.

Upgrading your skills or acquiring new skills will unveil new opportunities and help you find innovative solutions to problems. General skills, such as communication skills, writing skills, negotiation skills, etc., are very important in life. Continuous learning opens your mind and changes your attitude gradually by building on what you already know. The more you learn, the better you will be at seeing more sides of the same situation, which will help you understand more deeply.

You are in an era where knowledge is now at your fingertips. Those who are not using these resources will slowly diminish their capabilities and gradually become irrelevant. So, to remain relevant, you need to keep up to date with trends and adapt your skillset. To function effectively in this rapidly changing world of technology, you need to learn new things to remain valuable and with the flow.

Continuous learning helps you adapt to unexpected changes. By continuing to learn, you'll more easily step out of your comfort zone and take on new challenges with ease.

Learning helps to improve and grow in your career and helps throughout your life. Learning new things gives us a feeling of accomplishment, which in turn boosts our confidence in our capabilities. Acquiring new skills unveils new opportunities and helps you find innovative solutions to problems. This could earn you more money. Continuous learning opens your mind and changes your attitude by building on what you already know. The more you learn, the better you'll get at seeing more sides of the same situation, helping you understand more deeply. Continuous learning helps develop your leadership skills, which translates into fostering lifelong learning in other individuals by encouraging them to pursue further education.

## Why Apply?

Only learning adds knowledge and wisdom but applying those learnings in your life adds value. Successful people are fast implementers of whatever they have learned. They do not wait for the right moment to implement. Learning is very important; applying those learning in action is equally important. When learning and applying are congruent and go hand in hand, there is no stopping of progress. In other words, real progress happens when you learn things and apply them in your life toward achieving your goals.

Learn to take action. The longer you procrastinate, the higher the likelihood that you won't do something. Action is important for self-confidence to develop. With every small success, you will be learning to take bigger and better risks. "Often the difference between a successful person and a failure is not that one has better abilities or ideas, but the courage that one has to bet on one's ideas, to take a calculated risk – and to act" (Andre Malraux).

Do you think Michael Jordan never failed before? Here's what he said, "I've missed more than 9,000 shots in my career. I've lost almost 300 games. 26 times, I've been trusted to take the game-winning shot and missed. I've failed over and over and over again in my life. And that is why I succeed."

In other words, you must be ready to fail and to learn from your failures. You must turn your failures into feedback to help you grow.

Most people don't dare to take action because they are too afraid to fail. They let their fear of failure stop them from taking the necessary action.

When you fail, it's not the end of the day. You can start over and do it again. The bigger the failure, the higher the learning.

One of the biggest differences between someone successful and someone who is not is their ability to turn failure into success.

J.K. Rowling said, "It is impossible to live without failing at something. Unless you live so cautiously that you might as well not have lived at all, in which case, you fail by default."

**Action Point**

Make a habit of daily learning and apply that learning in life and business.

*"Success does not come from what you do occasionally, it comes from what you do consistently" - Marie Forleo*

Once a rich man requested a wise man to help his son to change his bad habits. The wise man asked the son to take a walk with him through the garden. After walking a few steps, the wise man stopped and asked the young man to pluck a small flower out of the ground.

The young man grabbed the plant with his fingers and easily plucked it out. The wise man nodded, and they resumed walking.

A few seconds later, the wise man stopped again and pointed towards another plant, a bit larger than the previous one. The young man grabbed it with his hand and plucked it out of the ground with a bit of effort. "Now pluck out that one," the wise man said, pointing towards a bush. The young man gripped the bush with both of his hands, and using all of his strength; he managed to pluck it out of the ground.

"Now you see that small tree, there? Try and pluck that one." The young man grabbed the trunk with both hands, pulled as hard as he could, but he couldn't even move it.

"It's impossible. I can't do it."

"You see, my boy, it's the same with our habits. If we let them grow and take root, it becomes harder and harder for us to stop them."

## How Habits Make The Difference

Habits make us who we are. Everything that you achieve in life is due to the habits that you have. Therefore, if you do not get the desired results, change your habits. In other words, habits will either make you or break you. Habits shape our lives far more than we probably realize. Habits are very strong. Our brains cling to them at the exclusion of all else—including common sense. It is said that more than forty percent of the actions a person performs each day are not actual decisions but habits. The habits grow stronger and stronger over time and become more and more automatic. So make sure you have developed the right habits.

## How To Create Habits

Two tadpoles, Ted and Todd, hatched from the same batch of eggs. They swam around excitedly, wiggling their little tails with great enthusiasm. They swam up to their mum and exclaimed, "Look what we can do, look why we can do." The mother frog looked at the two tadpoles with great pride and called them closer. She then explained the process of metamorphosis and how they will eventually lose their tail and grow legs.

This news impacted the tadpoles differently.

Ted was excited about the future and continued to swim with energy and enthusiasm, occasionally looking back to see when his legs would start forming.

Todd, however, thought to himself, "What's the point of exercising my tail? It's only going to drop off eventually anyway."

As a result, Ted kept strengthening his tail and increasing his stamina, but Todd's tail got weaker, and his energy levels dropped.

The mother frog took Todd to one side and suggested that he start using his tail more.

"But what's the point? It's only going to drop off anyway," Todd replied.

After a little while, the two tadpoles' tails dropped off, and their legs grew.

Ted was excited and hopped around with energy and enthusiasm. The consistent and energetic use of his tail had equipped him for this development.

Todd was less enthused. He was sort of glad that he now had legs, but he just didn't have the energy to use them.

He didn't know why; he just couldn't be bothered.

There are times in life when we are being prepared for the future, but it's not always in the ways we expect.

When we are learning calculus or ancient history in high school, we aren't learning it because we will use it, but because the skills learned will be valuable in the future.

When we start work, we do menial and low-level tasks, not because it's the best use of our skills or because it's what we learned to do in our previous studies, but because we will develop the necessary work ethic and level of initiative for later in our careers.

So the next time you think to yourself, "What's the point? I'm never going to use this in the future," remember the lesson of the two tadpoles.

Remember that the habits you form today will make a significant difference to your future success levels.[2]

Experts say that the best way to form a new habit is to tie it to an existing habit. So, observe the patterns in your day and think about how you can use existing habits to create new, positive ones.

---

2

https://betterlifecoachingblog.com/2013/01/04/the-two-tadpoles-a-story-about-creating-habits-for-the-future/

The morning routine is a great place to attach a new habit. A morning cup of coffee, for example, can create a great opportunity to start a new one-minute meditation practice. Or, while brushing your teeth, you can start walking for five minutes immediately after.

Dr. B.J. Fogg, the author of the book "Tiny Habits," described that big behavior change requires a high level of motivation that often cannot be sustained. He suggested starting with tiny habits to make the new habit as easy as possible in the beginning. In his own life, Dr. Fogg started with just two push-ups a day and, to make the habit stick, tied his push-ups to a daily habit of going to the bathroom. He began after a bathroom trip doing two push-ups. Now he has a habit of 40 to 80 push-ups a day. Habit researchers know people are more likely to form new habits when they clear away the obstacles that stand in their way.

**Action Point**

To form new habits, you connect them with an existing habit.

*"Consistent positive self-talk is unquestionably one of the greatest gifts to one's subconscious mind." – Edmond Mbiaka*

People are programmed to conducts many tasks or multitask but fail to find time for themselves or even conduct self-introspection. Self-talk is essential because what we talk, we manifest, and what we manifest, what we practice.

Life becomes enjoyable when we drive our own life ourselves, although it does not happen normally. In most cases, we do not know where we are heading; we leave it as such, we accept where it reaches. Those who want to control their lives and live a happy, healthy, and wealthy life have to pay attention to personal development, goals, and purpose and take action.

When people talk to the self, that talk goes to their subconscious mind and acts as a catalyst to remind us to work in that direction. Self-talk can be revisiting the goals and purpose, commitment to self, igniting passion, actions, etc. It creates a positive vibe in our minds to do the work.

**What Is Self-talk?**

Self-talk is the internal dialogue within the subconscious mind of an individual. Positive affirmations are great tools to counteract negative beliefs, thoughts, and self-talk. A conscious effort must be made to relinquish negative self-talk habits, and positive statements provide the revitalizing energy.

## How Self-talk Helps

Self-talk is the only talk where no one forces you to do something, and you can be yourself. It increases the ability to think more & dive deep into it, which directly leads to develop a strong, confident personality. We might not find a way every time, but it surely helps us in real-life scenarios. Small habits such as how you talk to yourself, the books you choose to read, whom you allow to have access to you that matter the most ultimately shapes your life.

Self-talk is rooted in your subconscious. It's nearly impossible to change without a little proactive rewiring.

The good part is that you can actually change the way you think by utilizing a very powerful affirmation technique. What has to happen is for your subconscious mind to change through the use of repetitive affirmation.

It means that you write out what you want to become in present tense form and read it out loud multiple times per day to yourself.

You need to do these all affirmations in the present tense as your subconscious mind won't react to future tenses. The real key here is repetition. Numerous studies have proven that through repetition, you can actually rewire the chemicals in your brain.

Secondly, to take this a step further, record yourself speaking this into your phone. You can also write down a list of all of the things you are currently struggling with, break them into bullet points and write how you want to address them in present tense form for each. It will be more effective if you record and listen to it daily multiple times.

## How to Overcome Negative Thoughts with Self-talk

It is key to explore the silent conversations we have with ourselves as they shape our lives, work, and relationships. Giving in to negative and disorienting self-talk—or "chatter"—can tank our health, sink our moods, strain our social connections, and cause us to fold under pressure.

Self-talk is something that happens and cannot be averted, and there is no need to avert also. Whenever we are having a conversation with ourselves, we tend to deep dive into a particular topic. Then we access them from many angles; if the topic is unhappy, negative thoughts are bound to come with prolonged thinking about it, but this is not the case when we are engrossed in thinking something 'good' or beautiful and happy moments. With the practice of mindfulness, the negative thoughts fade away and are gradually replaced with positive thoughts.

Second, if negative self-talk keeps spinning a negative story inside your mind, try to distance yourself from it while still learning more journalistic questions of "who, what, where, when, and why" to get a clear picture of the situation. Take a few moments to try to tell yourself the story of what happened as neutral as possible.

When you are doing self-talk, the third thing is to take it as if you are talking with Almighty. Whether you believe Him or not, imagine somebody supreme who is there with you, listening to you. When you are thinking negatively also with this background in mind, negativity will subside gradually.

The above three ways are very effective, and regular practice will make this a habit and reduce negative thoughts substantially.

**Action Point**

Practicing mindfulness can help you hear yourself and talk to yourself. When you notice negative self-talk in yourself, stop, consider it, evaluate its truth, and try a neutral or positive alternative.

Creating a life that is meaningful, joyful, and fulfilling is just like creating a good product. If you seriously work on the nine important elements covered in the book which helps to design your life in the early stage of life, viz., improve your self-talk, cultivate a growth mindset, improve risk-taking abilities, accept mistakes and move on, learn and apply, create new habits, think abundance, focus long term, think positive, that is very important to build their foundation for the future.

In order to know where you are going, you first need to know where you stand. Life is a balance across different areas, and one way to think about life is to divide it into pieces. There are no guarantees that life will turn out the way you want, but if you try, you have a better chance of it turning out in your way if you know how to design your own life.

In a nutshell, it's your life, and you call the shots to design your life. You control your life and what happens in it, and once you realize that fully, you give yourself room to grow, experiment, and begin designing the life of your dreams.

Are you ready to design your life? Yes, you can. Don't miss the opportunity; think in that direction and start working at whatever stages you are in at present. Sincere efforts towards this direction make your future better, brighter, and fulfilling. Good luck.

# 14.  Disclaimer

Although the publisher and the author have made every effort to ensure that the information in this book is correct, and while this publication is designed to provide accurate information regarding the subject matter covered, the publisher and the author assume no responsibility for errors, inaccuracies, omissions, or any other inconsistencies herein and hereby disclaim any liability to any party for any loss, damage, or disruption caused by errors or omissions, and whether such errors or omissions result from negligence, accident, or any other cause.

The ideas, procedures, and suggestions in this book are not intended as a substitute for consulting with an expert. Neither the author nor the publisher shall be liable or responsible for any loss or damage allegedly arising from any information or suggestion in this book.

Names, characters, and incidents in this book are either the product of the author's imagination or fictitious. Any resemblance to an actual person, living or dead, or actual events is purely coincidental.

## 15.  Copyright @ 2021 Pradip N Das

# 16.   Gratitude

This book is dedicated to my parents, wife, and son, whose continuous support helped me write another book on success.

I sincerely thank all my readers who inspired me with their love and appreciation for my previous books.

Jn

www.ingramcontent.com/pod-product-compliance
Lightning Source LLC
LaVergne TN
LVHW041223200726

843507LV00013B/2559